Northwoods Flannel
Quilts & Projects
BY DEBBIE FIELD FOR GRANOLA GIRL© DESIGNS

LANDAUER PUBLISHING

Northwoods Flannel
Quilts & Projects
BY DEBBIE FIELD FOR GRANOLA GIRL® DESIGNS

This book was designed, produced, and published by Landauer Books
A division of Landauer Corporation
3100 101st Street, Ste. A, Urbandale, Iowa 50322
www.landauercorp.com   800/557-2144

President/Publisher: Jeramy Lanigan Landauer
Vice President of Sales & Operations: Kitty Jacobson
Managing Editor: Jeri Simon
Art Director: Laurel Albright
Project Editor: Delores Farmer
Photographer: Sue Voegtlin

ISBN 13: 978-0-9818040-0-2
ISBN 10: 0-9818040-0-4

This book is printed on acid-free paper.

Printed in China

10 9 8 7 6 5 4 3 2 1

Northwoods Flannel Quilt & Projects by Granola Girl® Designs
Library of Congress Control Number: 2009927747

INTRODUCTION

Nestled in these pages are over a dozen easy-to-sew woodsy flannel quilts, throws, and projects to hunker down on those cool fall nights and cold winter days. You'll find easy-to-follow instructions so you can make the exact project, or, if you wish, see the sampling of wildlife appliqués and create your own irresistible snuggler.

I like to have a few homemade gifts on hand when friends and family visit. As we say our goodbyes, I send them on their way with a northwoods set of pillowcases or a candle mat so they will remember the good times we shared.

The two flannel fabric collections featured in this book by Debbie Field for Granola Girl® Designs are Tracks along the Trail and Tracking Whitetail Deer. Ask for them at your favorite quilt shop.

Take time for quilting and enjoy the outdoors!

Debbie Field

A special thank you to my creative friends for your individual talents.

Delores Farmer

Sue Carter

Cindy Kujawa

Jennifer Bauer

This book is dedicated to Sue Longeville, a friend who will be missed by all.

general instructions

Assemble the tools and supplies to complete the project. In addition to basic cutting and sewing tools, the following will make cutting and sewing easier: small sharp scissors to cut appliqué shapes, rotary cutter and mat, extra rotary blades, and a transparent ruler with markings.

Replace the sewing machine needle each time you start a project to maintain even stitches and to prevent skipped stitches and broken needles during the project. Clean the machine after every project to remove lint and to keep it running smoothly.

The projects shown are made with unwashed fabrics. If you prewash fabrics, purchase extra yardage to allow for shrinkage. The 100-percent flannels used in the wilderness quilts and accessories are from Debbie's Granola Girl® collections: Marblecake Basics, Tracking White Tail Deer and Tracks Along the Trail fabric lines manufactured by Troy Corporation. Ask for them by name at your local quilt shop.

Please read through the project instructions before cutting and sewing. Square the fabric before cutting by placing the folded fabric on your cutting mat. Align one of the horizontal lines on the ruler with the folded edge nearest you. Place your rotary cutter at the right edge of your ruler and cut fabric from selvage to selvage. Square your fabric again after cutting 3 or 4 strips.

To create accurate half-square triangles, align your ruler diagonally from corner to corner on each fabric square and cut.

Sew with 1/4" seam allowances throughout, unless stated otherwise in the instructions, and check seam allowance accuracy to prevent compounding even slight errors. Press seams toward the darker fabric when possible. When pressing small joined pieces, press in the direction that creates less bulk.

basic appliqué

Please note that the printed appliqué templates are reversed. Trace and cut the templates as printed, unless the illustrations and photos indicate to reverse the templates. For appliqués that face the opposite direction, trace and reverse the template. Dashed lines indicate design overlap.

Trace the appliqué template to the fusible webbing with a fine tip marker or sharp pencil, allowing space to cut 1/4" beyond the traced lines. Position the fusible web on the wrong side of the appliqué fabric. Follow the manufacturer's instructions to fuse the webbing to the fabric. Allow the fabric to cool and cut along the traced line. Remove the paper backing and follow the pattern placement to position the appliqué pieces on the background fabrics.

Use lightweight tear-away stabilizer to machine appliqué. Place the stabilizer beneath the fabric layers and use a small, zigzag stitch to sew around each shape, smoothly covering the raw fabric edge. The stitch is meant to secure the outermost edge of an appliqué shape in place. Your stitches should lie close together without appearing bunched up. If your machine has stitch options, use them to detail appliqués. After the stitching is complete, remove the stabilizer according to the manufacturer's instructions.

Paper Side of Fusible Web

Trace

Wrong Side of Fabric

Position and Fuse

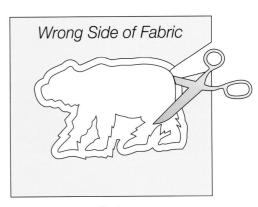

Wrong Side of Fabric

Cut

Peel

Right Side of Fabrics

Arrange and Fuse

basic binding

1. Cut the binding strips for your project from selvage to selvage. Join them for a continuous length by sewing the short ends of the binding strips, right sides together, with diagonal seams. Trim 1/4" from the sewn line and press open, as shown. Fold the strip in half lengthwise, wrong sides together, and press.

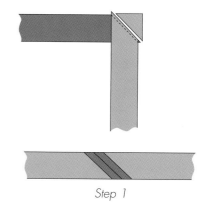

Step 1

2. Match the raw edges of the folded strip to the quilt top, along a lower edge and approximately 6" from a corner, allowing approximately 6" free to join to the opposite end of the binding. Avoid placing binding seams on corners. Sew the binding to the quilt top with a 1/4" seam allowance.

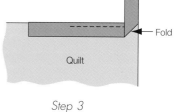

Step 2

3. At the first corner, stop 1/4" from the corner, backstitch, raise the presser foot and needle, and rotate the quilt 90 degrees. Fold the binding back onto itself to create a miter.

Step 3

4. Fold it along the adjacent seam, matching raw edges. Continue sewing to the next corner and repeat the mitered corner process.

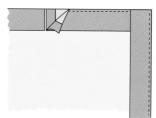

Step 4

5. Where the binding ends meet, fold under one binding edge 1/4", encase the opposite binding edge, and stitch it to the quilt top.

6. Trim the batting and backing fabric even with the quilt top and binding. Fold the binding strip to the back of the quilt and handsew it in place with a blind stitch. Sign and date the quilt, including the recipient's name if it is a gift.

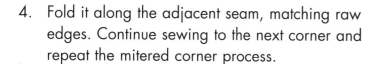

Step 5

basic quilting

- **Individual Motifs** Any design that stands alone, such as a flower or leaf, is a great choice for quilting the plain blocks in an alternating block quilt. You can often use a portion of an isolated motif to fill spaces in patchwork patterns. Designs along a border can also be repeated. Individual motifs can be square, circular, or oval—the range of possibilities is vast.

- **Stitching-in-the-Ditch** is stitching very close to the seams in a block. Patchwork blocks generally involve a lot of seam allowances. To avoid having to stitch through more layers than necessary with this type of block, try stitching in the ditch along the side of the seam with the least amount of bulk.

- **Outline Quilting** is a series of 1/4" stitching lines that outline the shape of the design in your block. You can choose to use this stitch to fill in the entire background section of your block.

- **Meander or Stipple Quilting** has an overall pattern that resembles the curvy pieces of a jigsaw puzzle. Ideally the quilting lines don't touch or overlap one another. It is a nice choice for covering large areas quickly or adding texture behind an appliqué shape to make it stand out.

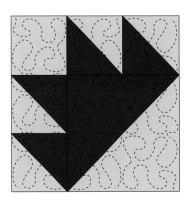

flannel helpful hints

Flannels have an approximate 2 percent or more shrinkage and will fray when pre-washed. If pre-washing flannel, purchase extra. Our instructions allowed for the 2 percent shrinkage, but please note not all flannels will shrink the same. This depends on the quality of the flannel you purchase.

If plaids pull out of shape during washing, realign the threads by pulling or tugging at the same time on opposite corners of the dried flannel.

For best results when quilting with flannels use large, simple, basic patchwork blocks like squares, triangles, or strip piecing.

Press flannel carefully; it is easy to stretch out of shape. To prevent stretching when piecing patchwork, use a slightly longer stitch length than normal. When machine patchwork piecing, take advantage of the flannel's stretchiness. Sometimes it is possible to stretch a slightly smaller piece to fit a larger one by placing the larger piece on the bottom as you sew. This allows the machine's feed dogs to help ease the pieces to fit.

appliquéing flannel

For best results always use a stabilizer that looks and feels like tissue paper. Do not use a stabilizer that is thick or stiff. A thick stabilizer will pull your stitches to the back of the quilt and pucker the appliqués when you try to remove it.

The purpose of a stabilizer when top stitching around an appliqué is to help prevent the fabric from jamming down into the feed dogs. It will show an even, consistent stitch, and let you glide around appliqués while zigzag stitching.

stitching around appliqués

A new needle is a must. For these projects I used an 80/12 needle and a slightly larger than normal zigzag stitch. I use Sulky® 40wt. Rayon thread. It is strong, shiny and is wonderful for appliquéing.

When choosing flannel for you quilts, keep in mind that some prints need to be next to a solid or plain flannel to calm the busier prints.

quilting

Since flannel is a heavier fabric, I recommend a low loft batting. When machine quilting use a longer stitch to prevent stitches from disappearing into the fabric weave.

THE SAMPLER QUILT

Materials

Finished size is approximately 62" x 78"

Refer to the General Instructions on pages 10-15 before starting this project.

7/8 yard Ecru Marble fabric for Star Block Background

1/2 yard Blue Tree fabric for Star Block Points

1/4 yard Gold Deer fabric for Star Block Center

1/4 yard Red Bear fabric for Star Block Center

1/4 yard Green Moose fabric for Star Block Center

7/8 yard Tan Antler fabric for Appliqué Background

7/8 yard Ecru Pine Cone fabric for Cabin Background

1/3 yard Brown Wood Grain fabric for Cabin Block

1/4 yard Light Brown Wood Grain fabric for Cabin Block

1-1/2 yards Dark Brown Wood Grain fabric for Cabin Roof, Sashing, and 1st Border

2-1/8 yards Green Marble fabric for 2nd Border and Binding

1/4 yard Green Marblecake fabric for Tree

6" x 6" piece Brown Wood Grain fabric for Tree Trunks

8" x 24" piece Gold Marblecake fabric for Deer

3" x 12" piece Dark Brown Wood Grain fabric for Antlers

1/4 yard Dark Green Marble fabric for Trees

7" x 8" piece Dark Brown Wood Grain fabric for Tree Trunks

10" x 16" piece Black Marblecake fabric for Door, Window Trim and Chimney

7" x 9" piece Gold Check fabric for Windows

5 yards fabric for Backing

70" x 86" Batting

Lightweight paper-backed fusible web

Lightweight tear-away stabilizer

Sulky® threads to match appliqués

Note: Fabrics are based on 42" wide fabrics that have not been washed. Please purchase accordingly.

Cutting Instructions

From Ecru Marble fabric, cut:
- 4 strips—2-1/2" x 42"; from these strips, cut: 60 squares—2-1/2" x 2-1/2".
- 5 strips—2-7/8" x 42"; from these strips, cut: 60 squares—2-7/8" x 2-7/8"; cut squares in half diagonally to make 120 half-square triangles.

From Blue Tree fabric, cut:
- 5 strips—2-7/8" x 42"; from these strips, cut: 60 squares—2-7/8" x 2-7/8"; cut squares in half diagonally to make 120 half-square triangles.

From Gold Deer fabric, cut:
- 5 fussy cut squares—4-1/2" x 4-1/2".

From Red Bear fabric, cut:
- 5 fussy cut squares—4-1/2" x 4-1/2".

From Green Moose fabric, cut:
- 5 fussy cut squares—4-1/2" x 4-1/2".

From Tan Antler fabric, cut:
- 2 strips—13-1/2" x 42".

From Ecru Pine Cone fabric, cut:
- 1 strip—7" x 42"; from this strip, cut: 2 rectangles—7" x 9-1/8".
- 1 strip—19-3/4" x 42"; from this strip, cut: 3 rectangles—19-3/4" x 8-1/2".

From Brown Wood Grain fabric, cut:
- 2 strips—3" x 42"; from these strips, cut: 6 rectangles—3" x 12-1/2".

From Light Brown Wood Grain fabric, cut:
- 2 strips—1-3/4" x 42"; from these strips, cut: 6 rectangles—1-3/4" x 12-1/2".

From Dark Brown Wood Grain fabric, cut:
- 3 strips—2-1/2" x 42"; from these strips, cut: 12 rectangles—2-1/2" x 8-1/2".
- 1 strip—8-7/8" x 42"; from this strip, cut: 2 rectangles—8-7/8" x 13-3/8".
- 12 strips—2-1/2" x 42".

From Green Marble fabric, cut:
- 8 strips—5-1/2" x 42".
- 8 strips—3" x 42".

Block Assembly

1. Sew together an Ecru Marble and a Blue Tree 2-7/8" half-square triangle, as shown. Press toward the dark. You will need 120 Unit A.

Unit A; Make 120

2. Sew 2 Unit A together, as shown. Press center seam open. You will need 60 Unit B.

Unit B; Make 60

3. Sew a 2-1/2" Ecru Marble square to each end of Unit B, as shown. Press toward the square. You will need 30 Unit C.

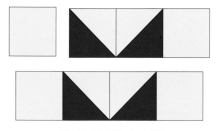

Unit C; Make 30

4. Sew a Unit B to each side of a fussy cut 4-1/2" square, as shown. Press seams toward center. You will need 15 Unit D.

Unit D; Make 15

5. Sew a Unit C to the top and bottom of Unit D, as shown. Press. You will need 15 Unit E.

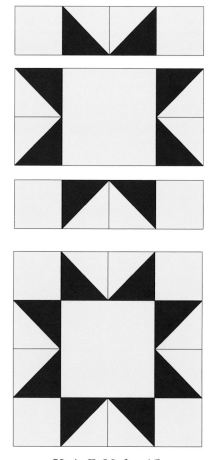

Unit E; Make 15

Star Row Assembly

Sew 4 Dark Brown Wood Grain 2-1/2" x 8-1/2" rectangles to 5 Unit E, as shown. Press toward the sashing.

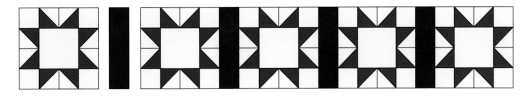

Deer and Tree Row Assembly

1. Sew the 2 Tan Antler 13-1/2" x 42" rectangles end to end. Press.

2. Cut 1—13-1/2" x 48-1/2" rectangle.

3. It is best to do the appliqué work at this time. Refer to the appliqué placement and the General Instructions on pages 10-11 to fuse and position the appliqué pieces to the background.

4. When placing the center deer appliqué piece to the background, start 1/2" to 3/4" from bottom raw edge.

5. Use a small zigzag stitch and matching thread around each shape to appliqué it to the background piece. Remember to use tear-away stabilizer when stitching appliqués.

Cabin and Tree Row Assembly

Note: Handle carefully, some pieces are on the bias

1. Sew 3 Brown Wood Grain 3" x 12-1/2" rectangles and 3 Light Brown Wood Grain 1-3/4" x 12-1/2" rectangles together, as shown. Press toward the dark. You will need 2 Unit A.

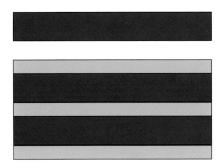

Unit A; Make 2

2. Fold each Dark Brown Wood Grain 8-7/8" x 13-3/8" rectangle in half widthwise so it measures approximately 8-7/8" x 6-11/16".

3. Place fold on left side and diagonally cut from upper left corner to bottom right corner, as shown. Discard the 2 loose triangles that were cut off.

Make 2

4. Place the Ecru Pine Cone 7" x 9-1/8" rectangles right sides together. Diagonally cut once and mark each section as #1 and #2, as shown.

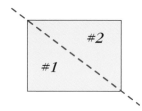

5. Sew both #1 triangles to each side of 1 Dark Brown Wood Grain triangle, as shown. Press toward the outside. Repeat using the #2 triangles on the remaining Dark Brown Wood Grain triangle.

Make 2

6. Sew the roof section to Unit A, as shown, to make a cabin block. Press toward the dark. You will need 2 cabin blocks.

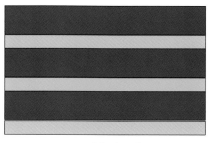

Make 2

7. Sew 2 cabin blocks and 3 Ecru Pine Cone 19-3/4" x 8-1/2" rectangles together, as shown. Press toward the rectangles.

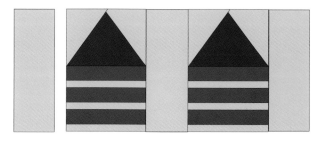

8. It is best to do the appliqué work at this time. Refer to the appliqué placement and the General Instructions on pages 10-11 to fuse and position the appliqué pieces.

9. Use a small zigzag stitch and matching thread around each shape to appliqué it to the background piece. Remember to use tear-away stabilizer when stitching appliqués.

Top Assembly

1. Diagonally piece and cut the Dark Brown Wood Grain 2-1/2" sashing strips into 6—2-1/2" x 48-1/2" strips.

2. Sew the 6 sashing strips, 3 star rows, deer/tree row and cabin/tree row together, as shown. Press toward the dark.

3. Measure the quilt top lengthwise through the center for the length of side border strips. Cut 2 strips the length needed from the Dark Brown Wood Grain 2-1/2" strips. Sew strips to each side of quilt. Press toward the dark.

4. Measure the quilt top widthwise through the center for the length of the top and bottom border strips. Cut 2 strips the length needed from the Green Marble 5-1/2" strips. Sew the strips to the top and bottom. Press toward the dark.

5. Measure the quilt top lengthwise through the center for the length of side border strips. Cut 2 strips the length needed from the Green Marble 5-1/2" strips. Sew strips to each side of quilt. Press toward the dark.

Finishing the Quilt

Layer the quilt backing fabric, batting and quilt top. Baste the layers together. Hand or machine quilt as desired. Finish the quilt by sewing on the binding following the steps in the General Instructions on page 12.

Deer Template
Cut 1 of Each

Deer Template
Cut 2 of Each

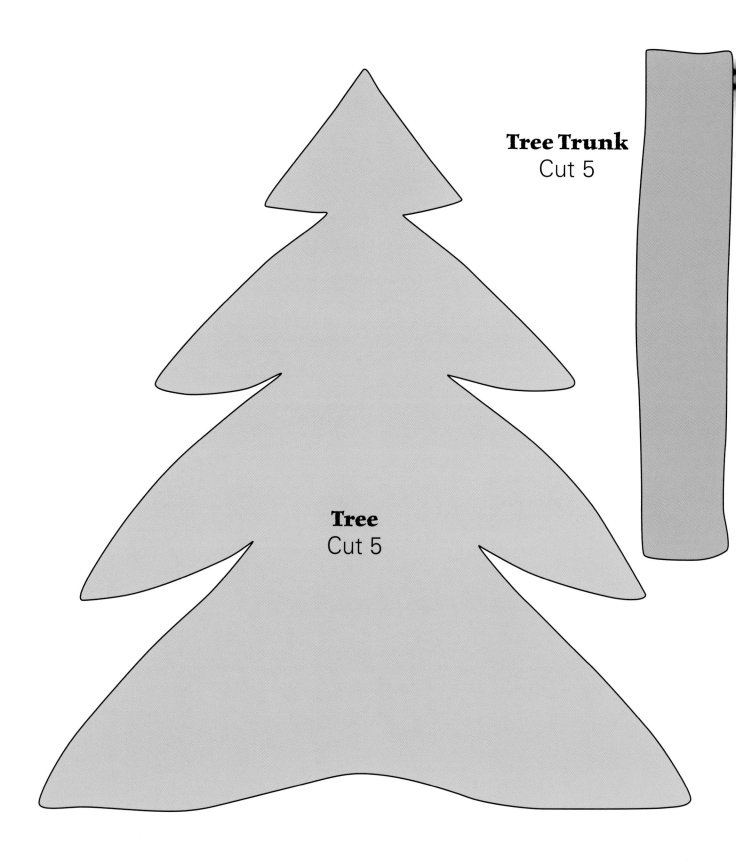

Tree Trunk
Cut 5

Tree
Cut 5

Tree Top
Cut 3

Tree Top Middle
Cut 3

Tree Top Bottom
Cut 3

**Window
Frame**
Cut 6

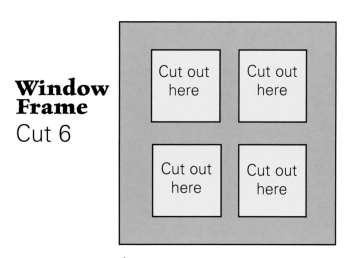

Cut out here

Cut out here

Cut out here

Cut out here

**Inside of
Window**
Cut 6

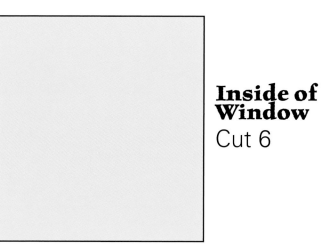

**Tree Trunk
Bottom**
Cut 3

Chimney
Cut 2

Door
Cut 2

**Tree Trunk
Top**
Cut 3

THE SAMPLER QUILT 62" x 78"

CHECKER GAME QUILT

Materials

Finished size approximately 56" x 88"

Refer to the General Instructions on pages 10-15 before starting this project.

5/8 yard Light Brown Wood Grain fabric for Center Checker Board Squares

1-1/2 yards Dark Brown Wood Grain fabric for Center Checker Board Squares and 3rd Border

3/8 yard Green Marblecake fabric for 1st Border

5/8 yard Blue Tree fabric for 2nd Border

2-5/8 yards Gold Deer fabric for 2nd Border, 4th Border, and Binding

3/8 yard Green Check fabric for Light Checkers

3/8 yard Navy Deer fabric for Dark Checkers

1 fat quarter Blue Tree fabric for Pouch

Black Ribbon or Jute as needed

5-3/4 yards fabric for Backing

67" x 97" for Batting, plus 28—3-1/2" x 3-1/2" pieces for checkers

Note: Fabrics are based on 42" wide fabrics that have not been washed. Please purchase accordingly.

Cutting Instructions

From Light Brown Wood Grain fabric, cut:
- 4 strips—4-1/2" x 42"; from these strips, cut: 32 squares—4-1/2" x 4-1/2".

From Dark Brown Wood Grain fabric, cut:
- 4 strips—4-1/2" x 42"; from these strips, cut: 32 squares—4-1/2" x 4-1/2".
- Cut 6 strips—4-1/2" x 42".

From Green Marblecake fabric, cut:
- 4 strips—2-1/2" x 42".

From Blue Tree fabric, cut:
- 4 strips—4-1/2" x 42".

From Gold Deer fabric, cut:
- 2 strips—8-1/2" x 42".
- 7 strips—6-1/2" x 42".
- 8 strips—3" x 42".

From Green Check fabric, cut:
- 3 strips—3-1/4" x 42"; from these strips, cut: 28 squares—3-1/4" x 3-1/4".

From Navy Deer fabric, cut:
- 3 strips—3-1/4" x 42"; from these strips, cut: 28 squares—3-1/4" x 3-1/4".

From Blue Tree fabric, cut:
- 1 rectangle—17" x 12".

Assembly Checker Board Center

1. Sew 4 Light Brown Wood Grain 4-1/2" squares and 4 Dark Brown Wood Grain 4-1/2" squares together as shown. Press toward the dark. You will need 8 Unit A.

Unit A; Make 8

2. Sew 8 Unit A together, alternating the Light Brown Wood Grain and Dark Brown Wood Grain squares to form the checker board center. Press in the direction of least amount of bulk.

1st Border

1. Measure the quilt top through the center lengthwise for side border measurement. Cut 2 strips from the Green Marblecake 2-1/2" strips to measured length. Sew strips to each side of the checker board center. Press toward the border.

2. Measure the quilt top through the center widthwise for top and bottom border measurement. Cut 2 strips from the Green Marblecake 2-1/2" strips to measured length. Sew strips to top and bottom of the checker board center. Press toward the border.

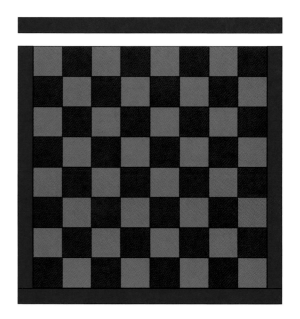

2nd Border

1. Measure the quilt top through the center widthwise for top and bottom border measurement. Cut 4 strips to the measured length from the Blue Tree 4-1/2" strips and 2 strips the measured length from the Gold Deer 8-1/2" strips.

2. Sew 2 Blue Tree 4-1/2" strips and one Gold Deer 8-1/2" strip together, as shown. Press toward the dark. You will need 2 Unit B.

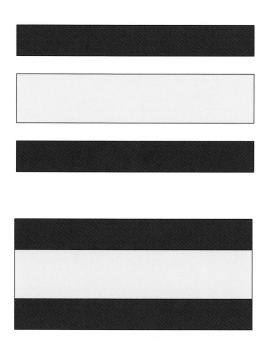

Unit B; Make 2

3. Sew a Unit B to the top and bottom of quilt top. Press toward the border.

3rd Border

Repeat steps 1 and 2 from the 1st border instructions using the Dark Brown Wood Grain 4-1/2" strips.

4th Border

Repeat steps 1 and 2 from the 1st border instructions using the Gold Deer 6-1/2" strips.

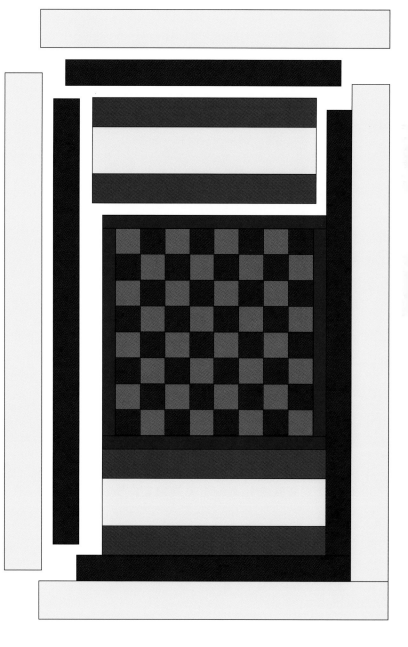

Finishing the Quilt

Layer the backing fabric, batting, and quilt top. Baste the layers together. Hand or machine quilt as desired. Finish the quilt by sewing on the binding following the steps in the General Instructions on page 12.

CHECKER GAME QUILT 56" x 88"

Checkers

With right sides facing, layer two 3-1/4" Green Check squares together and place on top of a 3-1/2" batting square. Stitch around edges leaving an opening on one side. Trim excess batting. Turn right side out and press. Hand sew opening closed. Top stitch 1/4" around each checker square. You will need 14. Repeat using the Navy Deer fabric. You will need 14.

Green Check Checkers; Make 14

Navy Deer Checkers; Make 14

Checker Pouch

Turn the Blue Tree fat quarter under 1/4" twice along one 17" side to create a finished edge. Top stitch and press. Fold in half and with right sides together, sew the remaining edges. Turn right side out and press. Tie closed with ribbon or jute.

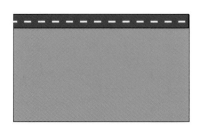

BEAR PAW QUILT

Materials

Finished size approximately 58" x 72"

Refer to the General Instructions on pages 10-15 before starting this project.

5/8 yard Blue Bear fabric
for Blocks and 2nd Border Squares

5/8 yard Red Bear fabric for Blocks

5/8 yard Tan Bear fabric for Blocks

1/3 yard Black Pine Cone fabric for Blocks

1/3 yard Blue Trees fabric for Blocks

7/8 yard Ecru Pine Cone fabric for Blocks

2-3/8 yards Brown Marblecake fabric
for Blocks, Corner and Setting Triangles, and Binding

5/8 yard Green Marblecake fabric for 1st Border

1-7/8 yards Directional Logs and Paws fabric
for 2nd Border
OR
1-1/8 yards Non-Directional Print fabric for 2nd Border

4 yards fabric for Backing

68" x 82" Batting

Note: Fabrics are based on 42" wide fabrics that have not been washed. Please purchase accordingly.

Cutting Instructions

From Blue Bear fabric, cut:
- 4 fussy cut squares—7-1/2" x 7-1/2".
- 4 fussy cut squares—5" x 5".

From Red Bear fabric, cut:
- 4 fussy cut squares—7-1/2" x 7-1/2".

From Tan Bear fabric, cut:
- 4 fussy cut squares—7-1/2" x 7-1/2".

From Black Pine Cone fabric, cut:
- 1 strip—7-1/2" x 42"; from this strip, cut:
  3 squares—7-1/2" x 7-1/2".

From Blue Tree fabric, cut:
- 1 strip—7-1/2" x 42"; from this strip, cut:
  3 squares—7-1/2" x 7-1/2".

From Ecru Pine Cone fabric, cut:
- 4 strips—4-3/8" x 42"; from these strips, cut:
  36 squares—4-3/8" x 4-3/8"; cut squares in half diagonally to make 72 half-square triangles.
- 2 strips—4" x 42"; from these strips, cut:
  18 squares— 4" x 4".

From Brown Marblecake fabric, cut:
- 4 strips—4-3/8" x 42"; from these strips, cut:
  36 squares—4-3/8" x 4-3/8"; cut squares in half diagonally to make 72 half-square triangles.
- 2 strips—16-1/8" x 42"; from these strips, cut:
  3 squares—16-1/8" x 16-1/8"; cut squares twice on the diagonal to make 12 quarter-square triangles.

Note: 2 quarter-square triangles will not be used.

- 1 strip—8-3/8" x 42"; from this strip, cut:
  2 squares—8-3/8" x 8-3/8" squares; cut squares in half diagonally to make 4 half-square triangles.
- 7 strips—3" x 42".

From Green Marblecake fabric, cut:
- 7 strips—2-1/2" x 42".

From Diagonal Logs and Paws fabric, cut:
- 4 strips—5" x length of fabric. Make sure to center design before cutting 2nd Border.

OR, if not using diagonal logs and paws fabric—

From Non-Directional Print fabric, cut:
- 7 strips—5" x 42".

Block Assembly

Note: Some pieces are on the bias, handle carefully.

1. Sew an Ecru Pine Cone and Brown Marblecake 4-3/8" half-square triangle together, as shown. Press toward the dark. You will need 72 Unit A.

Unit A; Make 72

2. Sew 2 Unit A together, as shown. Press in the direction of least amount of bulk. You will need 18 Unit B.

Unit B; Make 18

3. Sew 2 Unit A together, as shown. Press in the direction of least amount of bulk. You will need 18 Unit C.

Unit C; Make 18

4. Sew an Ecru Pine Cone 4" square to Unit C, as shown. Press toward the square. You will need 18 Unit D.

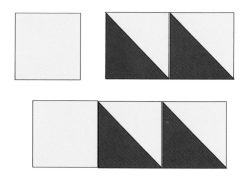

Unit D; Make 18

5. Sew a Unit B to a 7-1/2" print square, as shown. Press toward the square. You will need 18 Unit E.

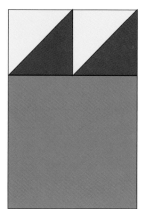

Unit E; Make 18

6. Sew a Unit D to a Unit E, as shown. Press in the direction with the least amount of bulk. You will need 18 Unit F.

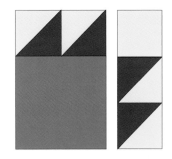
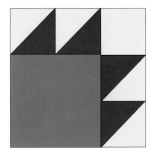
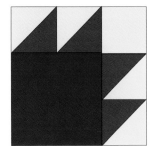
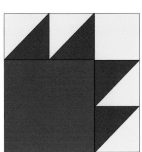

Unit F; Make 18

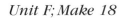

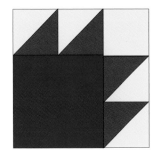

Quilt Top Assembly

1. Arrange the blocks in a pleasing order. Handle them carefully, some fabrics are on the bias and could stretch.

2. Sew the blocks, the 16-1/8" quarter-square triangles, and the 8-3/8" half-square triangles together, as shown. Mark each row as Row 1, Row 2, Row 3, etc. Press toward the blocks and triangles.

3. Sew the rows together, as shown. Press in the direction with the least amount of bulk. Square up the quilt top making sure to leave 1/4" seam allowance past each intersection.

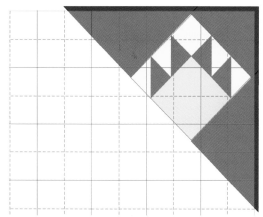

Borders

1. Measure the quilt top through the center widthwise for top and bottom border measurement. Cut 2 strips the measured length from the 2-1/2" wide Green Marblecake strips. Press toward the border.

2. Measure the quilt top through the center lengthwise for the side border measurements. Cut 2 strips the measured length from the 2-1/2" wide Green Marblecake strips. Sew the strips to each side. Press toward the border.

3. Measure the quilt top through the center widthwise for top and bottom border measurement. Record the length. Measure the quilt top through the center lengthwise for side border measurement. Record that length. Cut 2 strips from the Directional Logs and Paws 5" wide strips for the top and bottom length and cut 2 strips for the side border length.

4. Sew the top and bottom border strips to the quilt top. Press toward the border.

5. Sew a Blue Bear 5" square to each end of the side border strips, as shown. Press toward the dark. Sew side border strips to quilt. Press toward the border.

Note: If using a non-directional fabric repeat steps 3, 4, and 5 using the 5" wide Non-Directional Print.

Finishing the Quilt

Layer the quilt backing fabric, batting and quilt top. Baste the layers together. Hand or machine quilt as desired. Finish the quilt by sewing on the binding following the steps in the General Instructions on page 12.

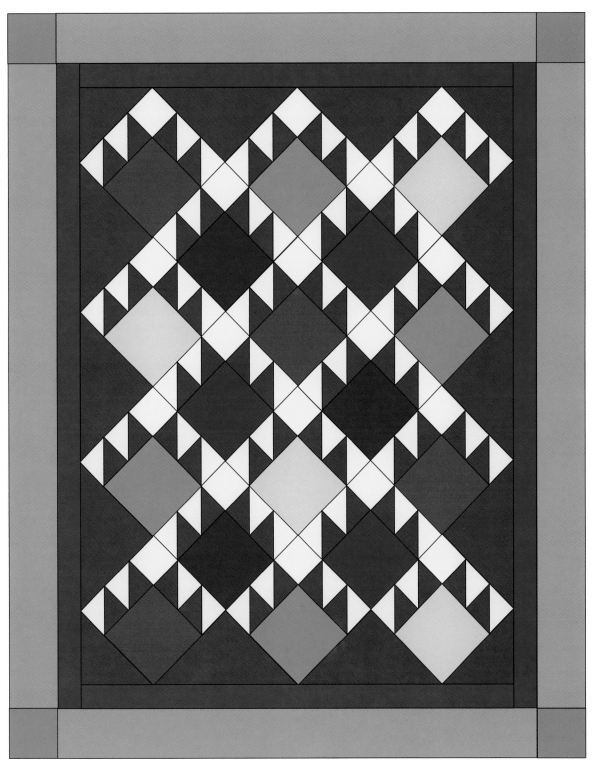

BEAR PAW QUILT 58" x 72"

PINE CONE TABLE RUNNER

Materials

Finished size approximately 19-1/2" x 60-1/2"

Refer to the General Instructions on pages 10-15 before starting this project.

3/4 yard Blue Pine Cone fabric for Blocks

2/3 yard Ecru Pine Cone fabric for Blocks

7/8 yard Green Marblecake fabric for Border and Binding

1-1/4 yards fabric for Backing

24" x 65" Batting

Note: Fabrics are based on 42" wide fabrics that have not been washed. Please purchase accordingly.

Cutting Instructions

From Blue Pine Cone fabric, cut:
- 2 strips—10-1/4" x 42; from these strips, cut: 4 squares—10-1/4" x 10-1/4".

From Ecru Pine Cone fabric, cut:
- 2 strips—11" x 42"; from these strips, cut: 4 squares—11" x 11"; cut squares twice on the diagonal to make 16 quarter-square triangles.

From Green Marblecake fabric, cut:
- 8 strips—3" x 42";

Block Assembly

1. With right sides facing, sew two Ecru Pine Cone quarter-square triangles on opposite sides of a Blue Pine Cone 10-1/4" square. Press. You will need 4 Unit A.

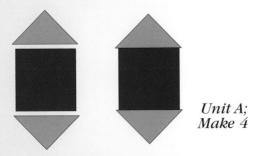

Unit A; Make 4

2. Sew two Ecru Pine Cone quarter-square triangles to opposite sides of one Unit A. Press. You will need 4 Unit B.

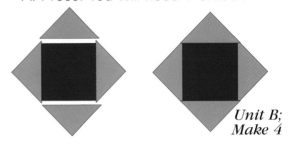

Unit B; Make 4

3. Sew 4 Unit B together, as shown, to make the table runner center.

Borders

1. Measure the short ends of the table runner center. Cut two 3" strips to the measurement and sew in place.

2. Measure the long sides of the table runner center. Cut two 3" strips to the measurement; you will need to piece the strips to get length needed. Sew strips in place on the table runner.

Finishing the Table Runner

Layer the backing fabric, batting and table runner top. Baste the layers together. Hand or machine quilt as desired. Finish the table runner by sewing on the binding following the steps in the General Instructions on page 12.

WHITE TAIL DEER LOG CABIN QUILT

Materials

Finished size approximately 95" x 116"

*Refer to the General Instructions
on pages 10-15 before starting this project.*

2/3 yard White Tail Deer Panel fabric for Center

3-1/8 yards Dark Brown Wood Grain fabric
for 1st and 3rd Border and Binding

3-1/4 yards Cream Camouflage fabric
for Log Cabin Blocks

1/4 yard Brown Wood Grain fabric
for Log Cabin Blocks

3/4 yard Gold Check fabric for Log Cabin Blocks

3-1/8 yards Black Deer Head/Leaf fabric
for Log Cabin Blocks and 5th Border

1-5/8 yards Green Camouflage fabric
for Log Cabin Blocks

10-1/2 yards fabric for Backing

King-size Batting

Note: Fabrics are based on 42" wide fabrics that have
not been washed. Please purchase accordingly.

Cutting Instructions

From White Tail Deer Panel fabric, cut:
- 1 rectangle—22-1/2" x 42-1/2".

From Dark Brown Wood Grain fabric, cut:
- 2 strips—5-3/4" x 42"; from these strips, cut:
  2 rectangles—5-3/4" x 22-1/2".
- 3 strips—5-1/4" x 42".
- 8 strips—5-3/4" x 42".
- 11 strips—3" x 42".

From Cream Camouflage fabric, cut:
- 55 strips—2" x 42"; from these strips, cut:
  52 squares—2" x 2".
  104 rectangles—2" x 5".
  104 rectangles—2" x 8".
  52 rectangles—2" x 11".

From Brown Wood Grain fabric, cut:
- 3 strips - 2" x 42"; from these strips, cut:
  52 squares—2" x 2".

From Gold Check fabric, cut:
- 10 strips—2" x 42"; from these strips, cut:
  104 rectangles—2" x 3-1/2".

From Black Deer Head/Leaf fabric, cut:
- 18 strips—2" x 42"; from these strips, cut:
  104 rectangles—2" x 6-1/2".
- 12 strips—5-3/4" x 42".

From Green Camouflage fabric, cut:
- 26 strips—2" x 42"; from these strips, cut:
  104 rectangles—2" x 9-1/2".

Assembly

1. Sew the 5-3/4" x 22-1/2" Dark Brown Wood Grain strips to the top and bottom of the White Tail Deer Panel, as shown. Press toward the border.

2. Measure the panel through the center lengthwise for side border length. Cut 2 strips from the 5-1/4" Dark Brown Wood Grain strips to that measurement. Sew to each side of the White Tail Deer Panel, as shown. Press toward the border.

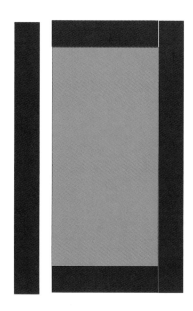

3. Sew a Cream Camouflage and Brown Wood Grain 2" x 2" square together, as shown. Press toward the Cream Camouflage. You will need 52 Unit A.

Unit A; Make 52

4. Sew a Gold Check 2" x 3-1/2" rectangle to Unit A, as shown. Press toward the outside. You will need 52 Unit B.

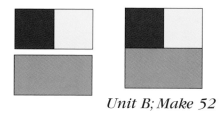

Unit B; Make 52

5. Sew a Gold Check 2" x 3-1/2" rectangle to Unit B, as shown. Press toward the outside. You will need 52 Unit C.

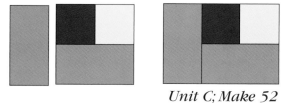

Unit C; Make 52

6. Sew a Cream Camouflage 2" x 5" rectangle to Unit C, as shown. Press toward the outside. You will need 52 Unit D.

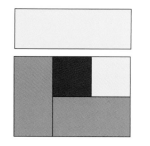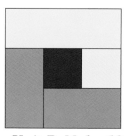

Unit D; Make 52

7. Sew a Cream Camouflage 2" x 5" rectangle to Unit D, as shown. Press toward the outside. You will need 52 Unit E.

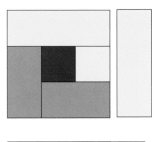

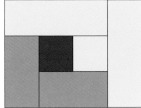

Unit E; Make 52

8. Sew a Black Deer Head/Leaf 2" x 6-1/2" rectangle to Unit E, as shown. Press toward the outside. You will need 52 Unit F.

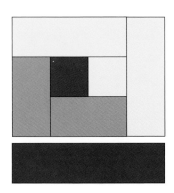

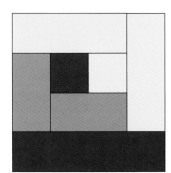

Unit F; Make 52

9. Sew a Black Deer Head/Leaf 2" x 6-1/2" rectangle to Unit F, as shown.

Press toward the outside. You will need 52 Unit G.

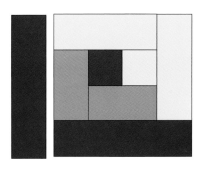

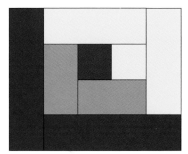

Unit G; Make 52

10. Sew a Cream Camouflage 2" x 8" rectangle to Unit G, as shown. Press toward the outside. You will need 52 Unit H.

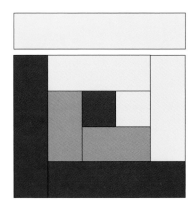

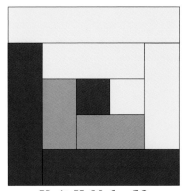

Unit H; Make 52

45

11. Sew a Cream Camouflage 2" x 8" rectangle to Unit H, as shown. Press toward the outside. You will need 52 Unit I.

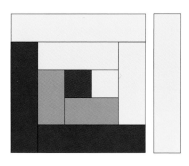

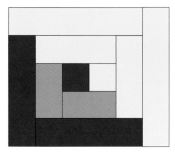

Unit I; Make 52

12. Sew a Green Camouflage 2" x 9-1/2" rectangle to Unit I, as shown. Press toward the outside. You will need 52 Unit J.

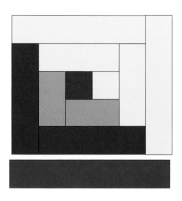

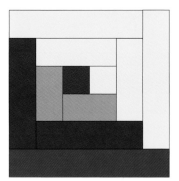

Unit J; Make 52

13. Sew a Green Camouflage 2" x 9-1/2" rectangle to Unit J, as shown. Press toward the outside. You will need 52 Unit K.

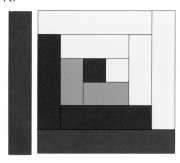

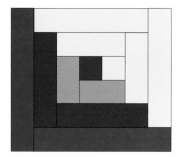

Unit K; Make 52

14. Sew a Cream Camouflage 2" x 11" rectangle to Unit K, as shown. Press toward the outside. You will need 52 Unit L.

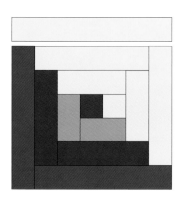

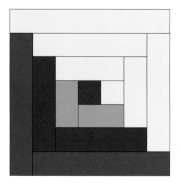

Unit L; Make 52

Quilt Assembly

1. Sew 3 log cabin blocks (Unit L) together, as shown. Press in the direction with the least amount of bulk. You will need 2 Unit A.

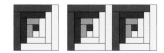

Unit A; Make 2

2. Sew 7 log cabin blocks together, as shown. Press in the direction with the least amount of bulk. You will need 2 Unit B.

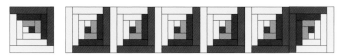

Unit B; Make 2

3. Sew a Unit A to the top and bottom of the quilt center, as shown. Press in the direction with the least amount bulk.

4. Sew a Unit B to each side of quilt center, as shown. Press in the direction with the least amount of bulk.

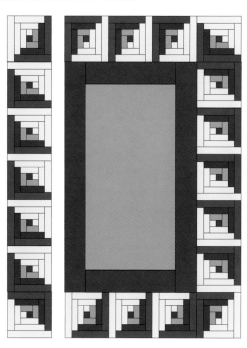

5. Measure the quilt top through the center widthwise for top and bottom border length. Cut 2 strips from the Dark Brown Wood Grain 5-3/4" wide strips to the length needed. Sew strips to top and bottom of the quilt top. Press toward the border.

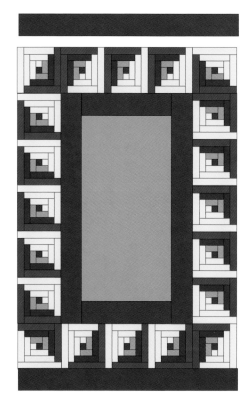

47

6. Measure the quilt top through the center lengthwise for the side border length. Cut 2 strips from the Dark Brown Wood Grain 5-3/4"-wide strips to the length needed. Sew strips to each side of quilt. Press toward the border.

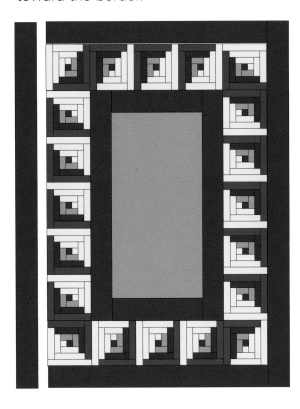

7. Sew 6 log cabin blocks together, as shown. Press in the direction with the least amount of bulk. You will need 2 Unit C.

Unit C; Make 2

8. Sew 10 log cabin blocks together, as shown. Press in the direction with the least amount of bulk. You will need 2 Unit D.

Unit D; Make 2

9. Sew a Unit C to the top and bottom of the quilt top, as shown. Press in the direction with the least amount of bulk.

10. Sew a Unit D to each side of the quilt top, as shown. Press in the direction with the least amount of bulk.

11. Measure the quilt top widthwise through the center for the length of the top and bottom border strips. Cut the length needed from the Black Deer Head/Leaf 5-3/4" wide strips. Sew the strips to the top and bottom of the quilt top. Press toward the dark.

12. Measure the quilt top lengthwise through the center for the length of the side border strips. Cut the length needed from the Black Deer Head/Leaf 5-3/4" wide strips. Sew to each side of the quilt. Press toward the dark.

Finishing the Quilt

Layer the backing fabric, batting, and quilt top. Baste the layers together. Hand or machine quilt as desired. Finish the quilt by sewing on the binding following the steps in the General Instructions on page 12.

WHITE TAIL DEER LOG CABIN 95" x 116"

In The Woods Quilt

Materials

Finished size approximately 68" x 84"

**Refer to the General Instructions
on pages 10-15 before starting this project.**

1/2 yard Tan Marblecake fabric
for Appliqué Background

1 yard Cream Tree fabric for Blocks

3-1/8 yards Green Check fabric
for Blocks, 2nd Border, and Binding

1 yard Light Brown Wood Grain fabric for Blocks

1 yard Black Moose fabric for Blocks

1 yard Black Marblecake fabric for 1st Border

3" x 4" piece Dark Brown Wood Grain fabric
for Tree Trunks

8" x 24" piece Light Green Marblecake fabric for Trees

8" x 24" piece Dark Green Marblecake fabric for Trees

8" x 10" piece Black Marblecake fabric for Bears

1" x 2" piece Gold Marblecake fabric for Bear Noses

8" x 8" piece Brown Marblecake fabric for Moose Body

4-1/2" x 4-1/2" piece Light Brown Wood Grain fabric
for Moose Antler

5-1/2 yards fabric for Backing

76" x 92" Batting

Lightweight paper-backed fusible web

Lightweight tear-away stabilizer

Sulky® threads to match appliqués

**Note: Fabrics are based on 42" wide fabrics that
have not been washed. Please purchase accordingly.**

Cutting Instructions

From Tan Marblecake fabric, cut:

- 1 rectangle—12-1/2" x 40-1/2".

From Cream Tree fabric, cut:

- 6 strips—4-7/8" x 42"; from these strips, cut:
  41 squares—4-7/8" x 4-7/8"; cut squares in
  half diagonally to make 82 half-square
  triangles.

From Green Check fabric, cut:

- 6 strips—4-7/8" x 42"; from these strips, cut:
  41 squares—4-7/8" x 4-7/8"; cut squares in
  half diagonally to make 82 half-square
  triangles.

- 8 strips—6-1/2" x 42".

- 8 strips—3" x 42".

From Light Brown Wood Grain fabric, cut:

- 6 strips—4-7/8" x 42"; from these strips, cut:
  41 squares—4-7/8" x 4-7/8"; cut squares in
  half diagonally to make 82 half-square
  triangles.

From Black Moose fabric, cut:

- 6 strips—4-7/8" x 42"; from these strips, cut:
  41 squares—4-7/8" x 4-7/8"; cut squares in
  half diagonally to make 82 half-square
  triangles.

From Black Marblecake fabric, cut:

- 7 strips—4-1/2" x 42".

Assembly

1. Sew a Cream Tree 4-7/8" half-square triangle and a Green Check 4-7/8" half-square triangle together, as shown. Press toward the dark. You will need 81 Unit A.

Note: 1 half-square triangle of each print will not be used.

Unit A; Make 81

2. Sew a Light Brown Wood Grain 4-7/8" half-square triangle and a Black Moose 4-7/8" half-square triangle together, as shown. Press toward the dark. You will need 81 Unit B.

Note: 1 half-square triangle of each print will not be used.

Unit B; Make 81

3. Sew 6 Unit B and 6 Unit A blocks together, as shown. Press in the direction with the least amount of bulk. You will need 7 Unit C.

Unit C; Make 7

4. Sew 6 Unit A and 6 Unit B blocks together, as shown. Press in the direction with the least amount of bulk. You will need 6 Unit D.

Unit D; Make 6

5. Sew 2 Unit A and 1 Unit B together, as shown. Press in the direction with the least amount of bulk. You will need 1 Unit E.

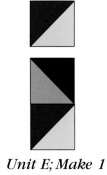

Unit E; Make 1

6. Sew 2 Unit B and 1 Unit A together, as shown. Press in the direction with the least amount of bulk. You will need 1 Unit F.

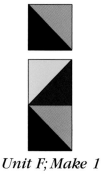

Unit F; Make 1

7. Sew 6 Unit C and 6 Unit D together, as shown. Starting with Unit C, alternate between Unit C and Unit D.

8. Sew Unit E to the left side of the Tan Marblecake 12-1/2" x 40-1/2" rectangle. Sew a Unit F to the right side. Press in the direction with the least amount of bulk.

9. Sew a Unit C to the top of the Unit E/Unit F Tan Marblecake background rectangle, as shown. Press in the direction with the least amount of bulk.

Appliqué

Note: *It is best to do the appliqué work on appliqué background border at this time. Refer to the appliqué placement and the General Instructions on pages 10-11 to fuse and position the appliqué pieces to the quilt top.*

1. When placing the appliqué pieces on the background, start 1/2" to 3/4" from bottom raw edge.

2. Use a small zigzag stitch and matching thread around each shape to appliqué it to the quilt top. Remember to use tear-away stabilizer when stitching appliqués.

Piecing the Quilt

Sew the Unit E/Unit F Tan Marblecake background rectangle to the top of the quilt top. Press in the direction with the least amount bulk.

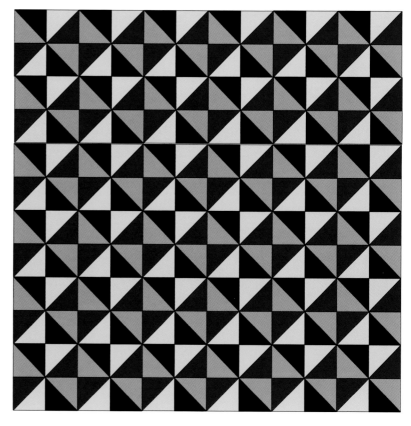

Border

1. Measure the quilt top widthwise through the center to determine the length of the top and bottom border strips. Cut strips the length needed from the 4-1/2" Black Marblecake strips. Sew the strips to the top and bottom of the quilt top. Press toward the dark.

2. Measure the quilt top lengthwise through the center to determine the length of the side border strips. Cut length needed from the 4-1/2" Black Marblecake strips. Sew onto each side of the quilt. Press toward the dark.

3. Repeat steps 1 and 2 using the 6-1/2" Green Check strips to make the 2nd border. Press toward the dark.

Finishing the Quilt

Layer the backing fabric, batting, and quilt top. Baste the layers together. Hand or machine quilt as desired. Finish the quilt by sewing on the binding following the steps in the General Instructions on page 12.

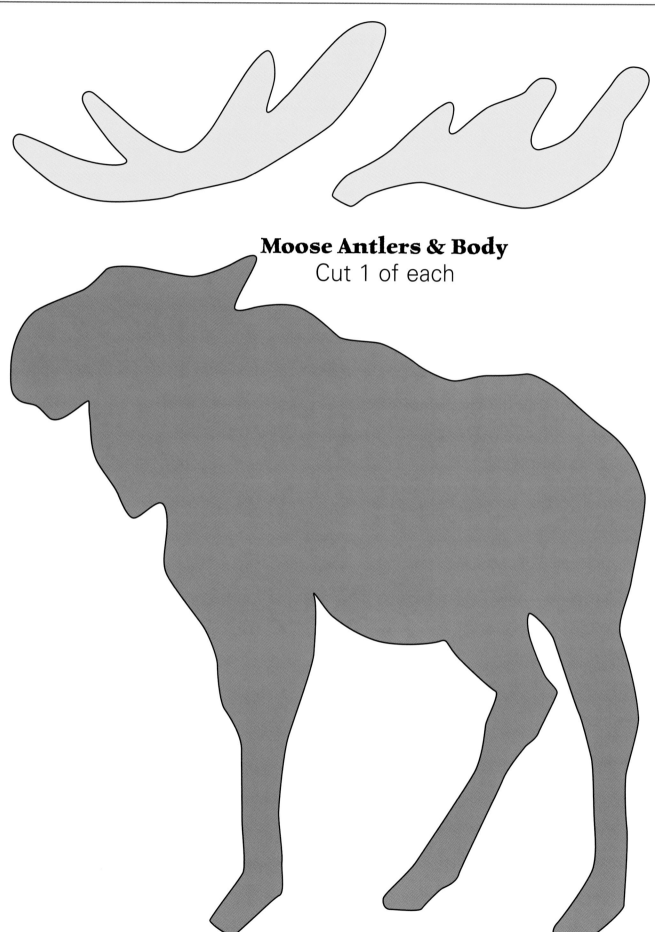

Moose Antlers & Body
Cut 1 of each

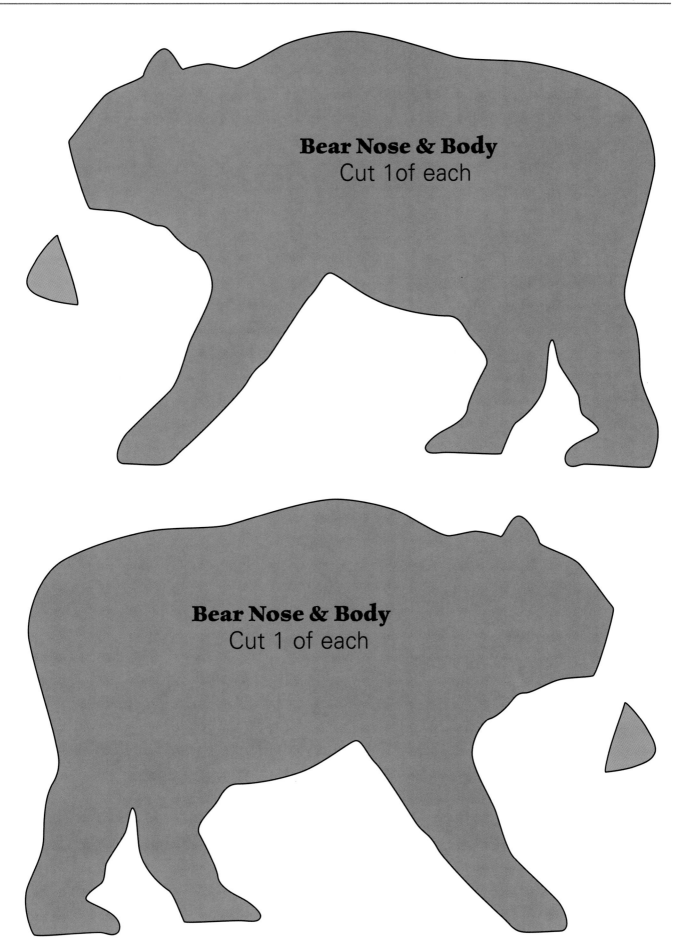

Bear Nose & Body
Cut 1of each

Bear Nose & Body
Cut 1 of each

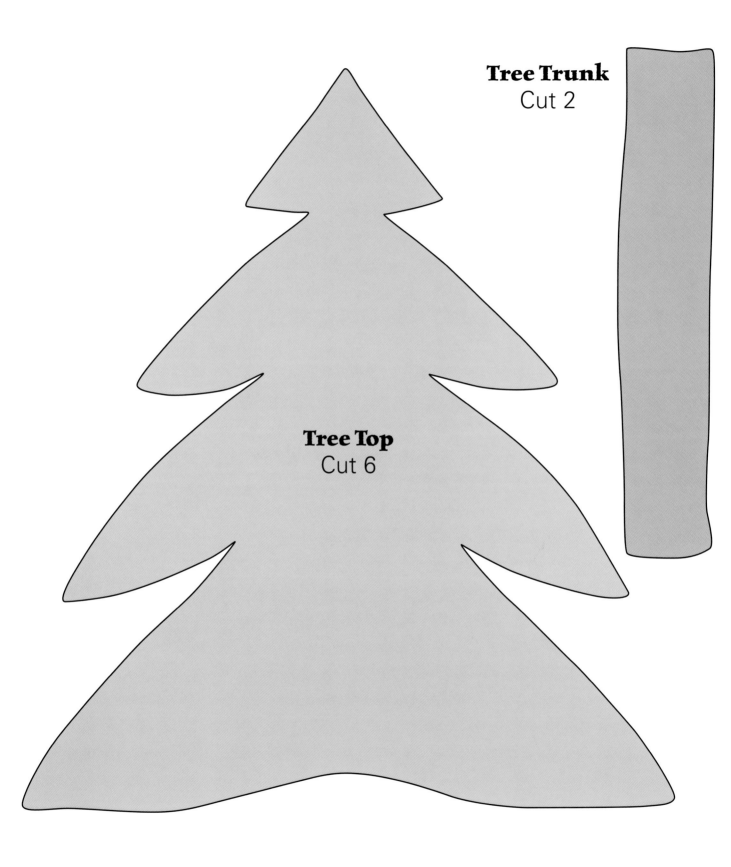

Tree Trunk
Cut 2

Tree Top
Cut 6

IN THE WOODS QUILT 68" x 84"

MOOSE TRACK SNUGGLER

Materials

Finished size approximately 60" x 76"

Refer to the General Instructions on pages 10-15 before starting this project.

1-3/8 yards Red Moose fabric
for Center and 2nd Border

1-3/8 yards Blue Wood Grain fabric
for 1st and 3rd Border

1 yard Tan Animal Tracks fabric for 3rd Border

2-1/8 yards Red Wood Grain fabric
for 4th Border and Binding

4-2/3 yards fabric for Backing

69" x 85" Batting

Note: Fabrics are based on 42" wide fabrics that have not been washed. Please purchase accordingly.

Cutting Instructions

From Red Moose fabric, cut:

- 1 rectangle—16-1/2" x 32-1/2".

- 5 strips—5-1/2" x 42".

From Blue Wood Grain fabric, cut:

- 3 strips—3-1/2" x 42";
  from these strips, cut:
  2 rectangles—3-1/2" x 16-1/2".
  2 rectangles—3-1/2" x 38-1/2".

- 6 strips—4-7/8" x 42";
  from these strips, cut:
  46 squares—4-7/8" x 4-7/8";
  cut squares in half diagonally
  to make 92 half-square triangles.

- 1 strip—4-1/2" x 42";
  from this strip, cut:
  4 squares—4-1/2" x 4-1/2".

From Tan Animal Tracks fabric, cut:

- 6 strips—4-7/8" x 42";
  from these strips, cut:
  46 squares—4-7/8" x 4-7/8";
  cut squares in half diagonally
  to make 92 half-square triangles.

From Red Wood Grain fabric, cut:

- 8 strips—6-1/2" x 42".

- 8 strips—3" x 42".

Assembly

1. Sew 46 Blue Wood Grain 4-7/8" half-square triangles and 46 Tan Animal Tracks 4-7/8" half-square triangles together, as shown. Press toward the dark. You will need 92 Unit A.

Unit A; Make 92

2. Sew together 8 Unit A, as shown. Press in the direction with the least amount of bulk. You will need 2 Unit B.

Unit B; Make 2

3. Sew 14 Unit A together, as shown. Press in the direction with the least amount of bulk. You will need 2 Unit C.

Unit C; Make 2

4. Sew 10 Unit A together, as shown. Press in the direction with the least amount bulk. You will need 2 Unit D.

Unit D; Make 2

5. Sew 14 Unit A together, as shown. Press in the direction with the least amount of bulk. You will need 2 Unit E.

Unit E; Make 2

6. Sew 2 Blue Wood Grain 4-1/2" squares and 14 Unit A together, as shown. Press in the direction with the least amount of bulk. You will need 2 Unit F.

Unit F; Make 2

7. Sew a 3-1/2" x 16-1/2" Blue Wood Grain rectangle to the top and bottom of the Red Moose quilt center, as shown. Press toward the border.

8. Sew A Blue Wood Grain 3-1/2" x 38-1/2" rectangle to each side of quilt top. Press toward the border.

9. Measure the quilt top through the center widthwise for the top and bottom border measurements. Cut 2 Red Moose 5-1/2" wide strips to the length needed. Sew strips to top and bottom of the quilt top. Press toward the border.

Pieced Border Assembly

1. Sew Unit B to top and bottom of the quilt top, as shown. Press in the direction with the least amount of bulk.

10. Measure the quilt top through the center lengthwise for the side border measurements. Cut 2 Red Moose 5-1/2" wide strips to the length needed. Sew strips to each side of the quilt top. Press toward the border.

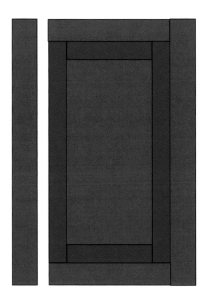

2. Sew Unit C to each side of the quilt top, as shown. Press in the direction with the least amount of bulk.

3. Sew a Unit D to the top and bottom of the quilt top. Sew a Unit F to each side, as shown. Press in the direction with the least amount of bulk.

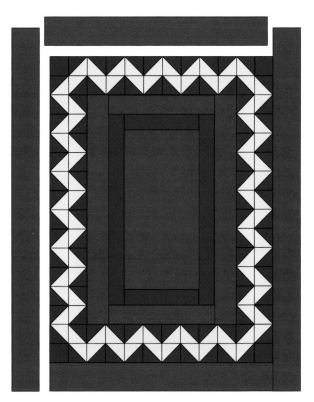

4. Measure the quilt top through the center widthwise for the top and bottom border measurements. Cut 2 Red Wood Grain 6-1/2"-wide strips to the length needed. Sew to the top and bottom of the quilt top. Press toward the border.

5. Measure the quilt top through the center lengthwise for the side border measurements. Cut 2 Red Wood Grain 6-1/2"-wide strips to the length needed. Sew to the top and bottom of the quilt top. Press toward the border.

Finishing the Quilt

Layer the backing fabric, batting, and quilt top. Baste the layers together. Hand or machine quilt as desired. Finish the quilt by sewing on the binding following the steps in the General Instructions on page 12.

MOOSE TRACK SNUGGLER 60" x 76"

Pine Cone Quilt

Materials

Finished size approximately 63" x 71"

**Refer to the General Instructions
on pages 10-15 before starting this project.**

3/4 yard Tan Marblecake fabric for Blocks

3-1/8 yards Black Pine Cone fabric
for Blocks, 3rd Border, and Binding

1/3 yard Green Marblecake fabric for 1st Border

1-5/8 yards Gold Check fabric for 2nd Border

1/2 yard Dark Green Marblecake fabric for Sprigs

18" x 18" piece Brown Marblecake fabric
for Pine Cones

4 yards fabric for Backing

72" x 80" Batting

Lightweight paper-backed fusible web

Lightweight tear-away stabilizer

Sulky® threads to match appliqués

Note: Fabrics are based on 42" wide fabrics that have
not been washed. Please purchase accordingly.

Cutting Instructions

From Tan Marblecake fabric, cut:
- 5 strips—4-1/2" x 42"; from these strips, cut:
  40 squares—4-1/2" x 4-1/2".

From Black Pine Cone fabric, cut:
- 5 strips—8-1/2" x 42"; from these strips, cut:
  20 squares—8-1/2" x 8-1/2".
- 7 strips—6" x 42".
- 7 strips—3" x 42".

From Green Marblecake fabric, cut:
- 4 strips—2" x 42".

From Gold Check fabric, cut:
- 6 strips—8-1/2" x 42".

Block Assembly

1. Draw a diagonal line on the back of the Tan Marblecake 4-1/2" x 4-1/2" squares.

2. Place a Tan Marblecake 4-1/2" square on opposite corners of a Black Pine Cone 8-1/2" square. Sew on the diagonal line. Press the Tan Marblecake square toward the outside. Trim away the center Tan Marblecake triangle only. You will need 20 blocks.

Make 20

3. Sew the blocks in rows of 4, as shown. Press in the direction with the least amount of bulk. You will need 5 rows of 4 blocks.

Make 5 rows

4. Sew the rows together, as shown. Press in the direction with the least amount of bulk.

Borders

1. Measure the quilt top through the center lengthwise for the side border measurements. Cut the 2" wide Green Marblecake strips to the length needed. Sew the strips to each side of the quilt top. Press toward the dark.

2. Measure the quilt top through the center widthwise for the top and bottom border measurements. Cut the 2"-wide Green Marblecake strips to the length needed. Sew the strips to the top and bottom of the quilt top. Press toward the dark.

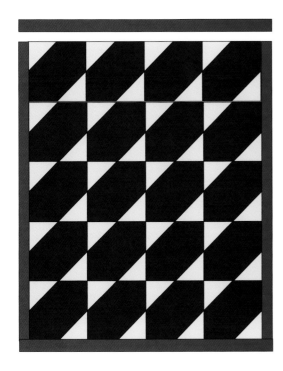

3. Repeat steps 1 and 2 for the Gold Check 2nd border and the Black Pine Cone 3rd border.

Appliqués

Refer to the appliqué placement and the General Instructions on pages 10-11 to fuse and position the appliqué pieces to the quilt top. Use a small zigzag stitch and matching thread around each shape to appliqué it to the quilt top. Remember to use tear-away stabilizer when stitching appliqués.

Finishing the Quilt

Layer the backing fabric, batting, and quilt top. Baste the layers together. Hand or machine quilt as desired. Finish the quilt by sewing on the binding following the steps in the General Instructions on page 12.

Pine Cone Sprig
Cut 10 & 10 reversed

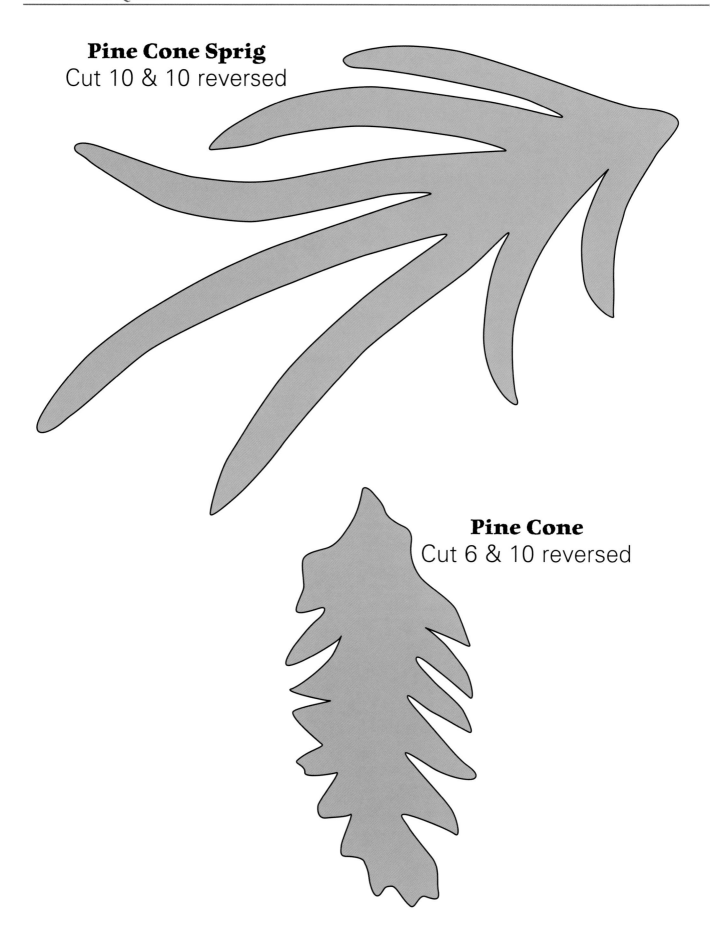

Pine Cone
Cut 6 & 10 reversed

PINE CONE QUILT 63" x 71"

CANDLE MAT

Materials

Finished size approximately 20-1/2" x 20-1/2"

Refer to the General Instructions on pages 10-15 before starting this project.

12" x 12" piece Black Moose fabric for Center Square Block

2 —15" x 15" pieces Ecru Wood Grain fabric for Setting Triangles and Backing

1/2 yard Dark Brown Wood Grain fabric for Tongues

Note: Fabrics are based on 42" wide fabrics that have not been washed. Please purchase accordingly.

Cutting Instructions

From Black Moose fabric, cut:

• 1 square—10-1/4" x 10-1/4".

From Ecru Wood Grain fabric, cut:

• 1 square—11" x 11"; cut square twice on the diagonal to make 4 quarter-square triangles.

From Dark Brown Wood Grain fabric, cut:

• 40 tongues (20 sets) using the template.

TONGUE
CUT 40

Assembly

1. With right sides facing, sew two Ecru Wood Grain quarter-square triangles on opposite sides of a Black Moose 10-1/4" square. Press.

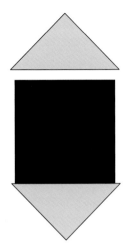

2. Sew two Ecru Wood Grain quarter-square triangles to the remaining sides of the square. Press.

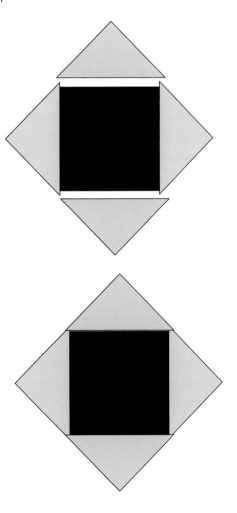

3. With right sides together, stitch around each **set** of tongues using a 1/4" seam allowance. Slightly clip top curve of each tongue. Turn right sides out and press. Top stitch around each tongue with a 1/4" seam allowance.

4. With right side of candle mat top facing up, place 5 tongues on each side, as shown. Baste 1/8" in from the outer edge to secure tongues in place.

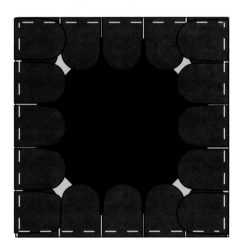

5. With right sides together, place the 15" x 15" Ecru Wood Grain backing on top of the candle mat top. Pin and stitch around the mat using a 1/4" seam allowance leaving a 4" opening.

6. Turn right side out and press. Hand sew the opening closed. Top stitch 1/4" around mat with a zigzag stitch.

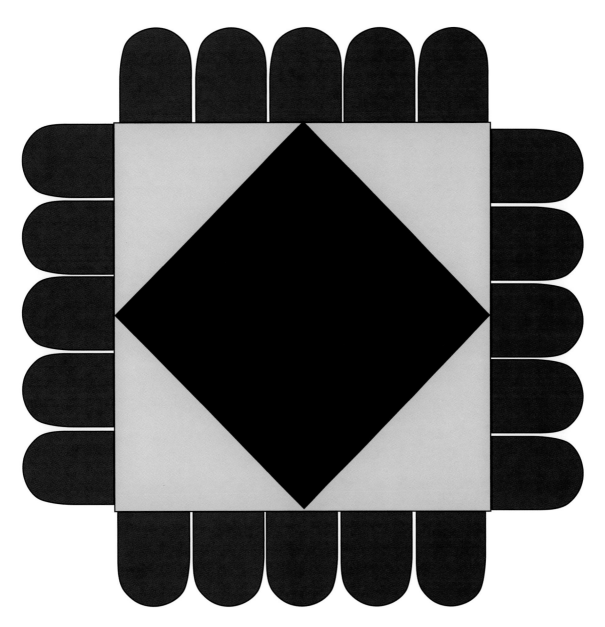

CANDLE MAT 20-1/2" x 20-1/2"

One Log At A Time Quilt

Materials

Finished size approximately 70" x 70"

Refer to the General Instructions on pages 10-15 before starting this project.

3/8 yard *each* 15 Coordinating Print fabrics for Center and 2nd Border

1/3 yard *each* 3 Light Print fabrics for 2nd Border

2-1/3 yards Navy Marblecake fabric for 1st and 3rd Borders and Binding

4-1/3 yards fabric for Backing

78" x 78" Batting

Notes: Fabrics are based on 42" wide fabrics that have not been washed. Please purchase accordingly.

Cutting Instructions

From *each* of the 15 Coordinating Print fabrics, cut:
- 2 strips—2-1/2" x 42"; from strips, cut:
  10 rectangles—2-1/2" x 6-1/2". You will need 140 total. *10 rectangles will not be used.*

From *each* of 12 of the Darkest 15 Coordinating Print fabrics, cut:
- 2 strips—2-1/2" x 42"; from strips, randomly cut:
  24 rectangles—2-1/2" x 8-1/2".
  24 rectangles—2-1/2" x 6-1/2".
  24 rectangles—2-1/2" x 5-1/2".
  24 rectangles—2-1/2" x 4-1/2".
  12 rectangles—2-1/2" x 3-1/2".

From each of the 3 Light Print fabrics, cut:
- 3 strips—2-1/2" x 42"; from strips, randomly cut:
  24 squares—2-1/2" x 2-1/2".
  24 rectangles—2-1/2" x 3-1/2".
  24 rectangles—2-1/2" x 4-1/2".
  12 rectangles—2-1/2" x 5-1/2".

From Navy Marblecake fabric, cut:
- 2 strips—2-1/2" x 42".
- 3 strips—3-1/2" x 42".
- 8 strips—4-1/2" x 42".
- 8 strips—3" x 42".

Assembly

1. Randomly sew 2 coordinating print 2-1/2" x 6-1/2" rectangles together, as shown. Press toward the dark. You will need 28 Unit A.

Unit A; Make 28

2. Randomly sew 3 coordinating print 2-1/2" x 6-1/2" rectangles together, as shown. Press toward the dark. You will need 28 Unit B.

Unit B; Make 28

3. Arrange 4 Unit A and 4 Unit B in a pleasing manner. Sew together, as shown. Press in the direction with the least amount of bulk. You will need 4 Row C.

Row C; Make 4

4. Arrange 4 Unit B and 4 Unit A in a pleasing manner. Sew together, as shown. Press in the direction with the least amount of bulk. You will need 3 Row D.

Row D; Make 3

5. Sew together Rows C and D, beginning with a Row C. Alternate rows and end with a Row C. Press in the direction with the least amount bulk.

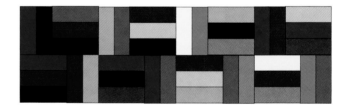

6. Measure the quilt top through the center widthwise for the top and bottom border measurements. Cut 2 Navy Marblecake 2-1/2"-wide strips to the length needed. Sew the strips to the top and bottom of the quilt top. Press toward the border.

7. Measure the quilt top through the center lengthwise for the side border measurements. Cut 2 Navy Marblecake 3-1/2"-wide strips to the length needed. Sew to the sides of the quilt top. Press toward the border.

Pieced Border

1. Randomly sew the 24 Light Print 2-1/2" x 2-1/2" squares to the 24 Darkest Coordinating Print 2-1/2" x 6-1/2" rectangles, as shown. Press toward the dark. You will need 24 Unit E.

Unit E; Make 24

2. Randomly sew the 24 Light Print 2-1/2" x 3-1/2" rectangles to the 24 Darkest Coordinating Print 2-1/2" x 5-1/2" rectangles, as shown. Press toward the dark. You will need 24 Unit F.

Unit F; Make 24

3 Randomly sew the 24 Light Print 2-1/2" x 4-1/2" rectangles to the 24 Darkest Coordinating Print 2-1/2" x 4-1/2" rectangles, as shown. Press toward the dark. You will need 24 Unit G.

Unit G; Make 24

4. Randomly sew the 12 Light Print 2-1/2" x 5-1/2" rectangles to the 12 Darkest Coordinating Print 2-1/2" x 3-1/2" rectangles, as shown. Press toward the dark. You will need 12 Unit H.

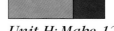

Unit H; Make 12

5. The 24 Darkest Coordinating Print 2-1/2" x 8-1/2" rectangles are referred to as Unit I.

Unit I

6. Sew together 4 Unit E, 6 Unit F, 6 Unit G, 3 Unit H, and 4 Unit I, as shown. Begin with a Unit F and create a "stepping" pattern. Press toward the dark. You will need 2 Row J.

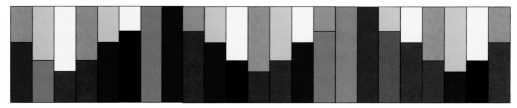

Row J; Make 2

7. Sew together 8 Unit E, 6 Unit F, 6 Unit G, 3 Unit H, and 8 Unit I, as shown. Press toward the dark. You will need 2 Row K.

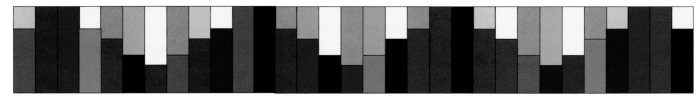

Row K; Make 2

8. Sew a Row J to the top and bottom of the quilt top with the light prints toward the center. Press toward the border.

9. Sew a Row K to each side of the quilt top with the light prints toward the center. Press toward the border.

10. Using the Navy Marblecake 4-1/2" strips, attach the border in the same manner as the 2-1/2"-wide Navy Marblecake border (see steps 6 and 7 under Assembly). Press toward the border.

Finishing the Quilt

Layer the quilt backing fabric, batting and quilt top. Baste the layers together. Hand or machine quilt as desired. Finish the quilt by sewing on the binding following the steps in the General Instructions on page 12.

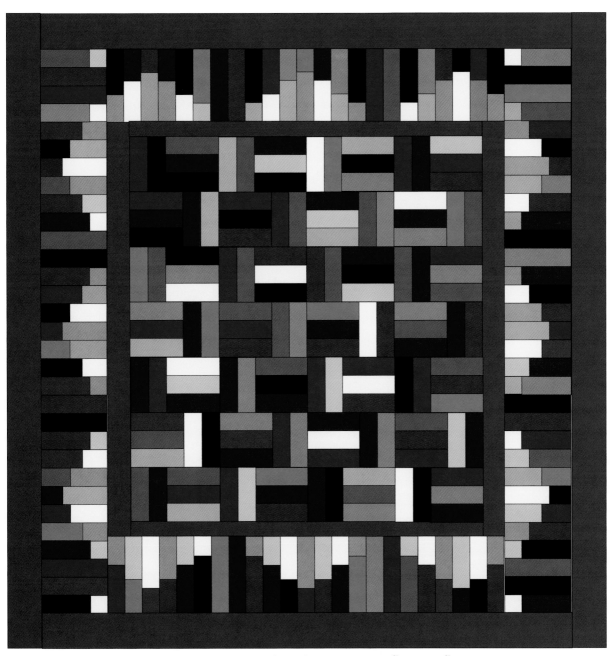

ONE LOG AT A TIME 70" x 70"

PILLOWCASE

Materials

Finished size approximately 19" x 30"

Refer to the General Instructions on pages 10-15 before starting this project.

Yardage amount is for 1 Pillowcase

7/8 yard Theme Print fabric for Body of Pillowcase

1/3 yard Coordinating Print fabric for Band of Pillowcase

Note: Fabrics are based on 42" wide fabrics that have not been washed. Please purchase accordingly.

Cutting Instructions

From Theme Print fabric, cut:
- 1 rectangle—27" x 40".

From Coordinating Print fabric, cut:
- 1 rectangle—9" x 40".

Note: A 1/2" wide seam allowance was used throughout this project

Assembly

1. Sew the 9" x 40" Coordinating Print rectangle to the 27" x 40" Theme Print rectangle, as shown. Press toward the band.

2. Fold the pillowcase in half widthwise with right sides together. Sew on 2 edges, as shown.

3. Press under 1/2" on band edge of pillowcase. Fold band in half with wrong sides together. Pin the folded edge of band to seam allowance. Top stitch band in place.

4. Turn pillowcase right side out and press.

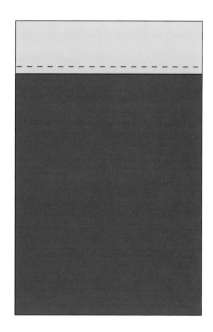

Suggestions:

To help prevent seam allowances from raveling try one of the following:

- Serge seams with a serger
- Machine zig-zag
- Use a zig-zag rotary blade
- Use pinking shears
- Use a decorative stitch on edge of band

FLANNEL TRIM

Materials

A full size sheet was used in this project.

A flat sheet in desired size—pre-wash and press.

Measure the length of the top band on your flat sheet to determine the amount of Flannel fabric you will need.

Example: If the band measured 4-1/4" in width, you would take that measurement times two for a total of 8-1/2". Then add 1/2" seam allowance to fold under on each raw edge of band. Cut Flannel strips 9-1/2" by width of fabric.

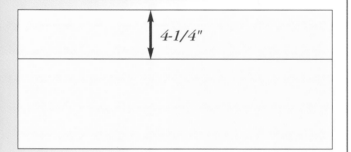

Cutting and Assembly

1. Measure top band of your flat sheet. Cut required amount of strips for that measurement. Piece strips together end to end for one continuous strip.

Example: For a full size flat sheet that measured 81", cut 2—9-1/2" x 42" strips. Add 1" to the 81" for folding over 1/2" on each end.

2. Fold the pieced strips over 1/2" widthwise on raw edges. Press.

3. Fold over 1/2" on each end. Press.

4. Fold strip in half and press. Overlap flannel strip covering sheet band. Pin in place and top stitch with a zigzag stitch across the width of sheet.

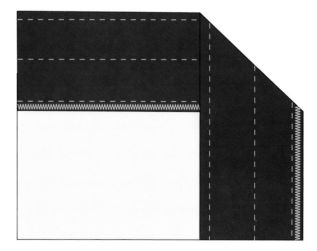

On the following pages you will find optional appliqué templates that can be used in place of templates in The Sampler (page 16) & In The Woods (page 50) projects. Just arrange in a manner pleasing to you and appliqué as instructed on pages 10 and 11.

Template options & placement for The Sampler Quilt (page 16) & In The Woods Quilt (page 50)

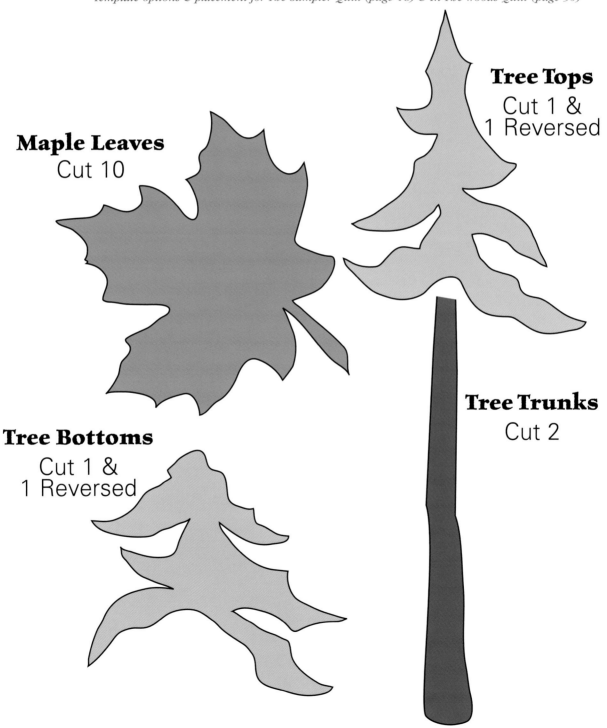

Tree Tops
Cut 1 &
1 Reversed

Maple Leaves
Cut 10

Tree Trunks
Cut 2

Tree Bottoms
Cut 1 &
1 Reversed

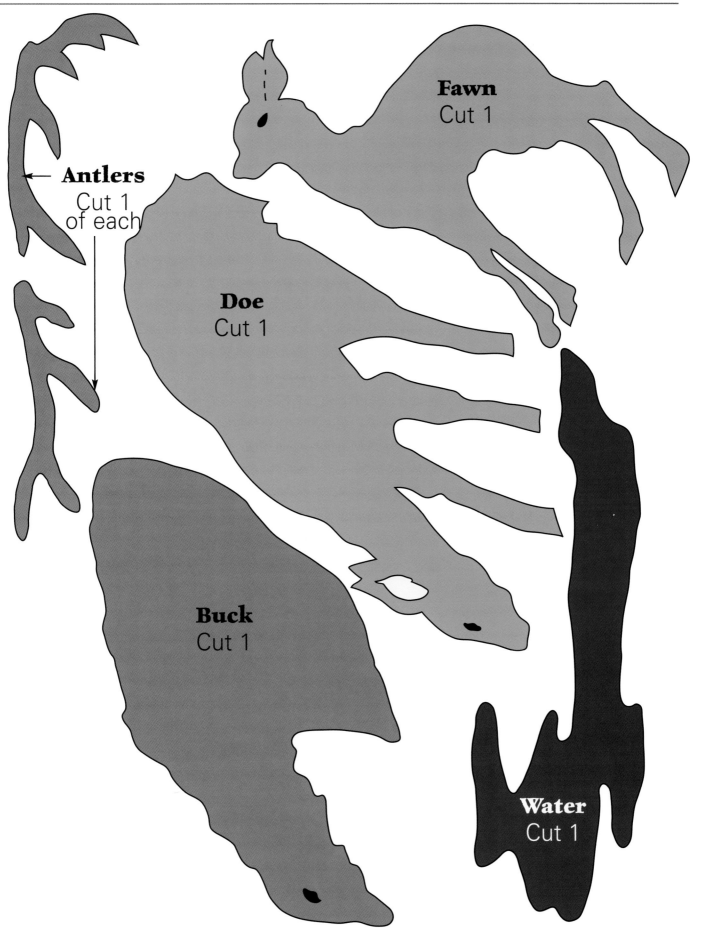

Antlers
Cut 1
of each

Fawn
Cut 1

Doe
Cut 1

Buck
Cut 1

Water
Cut 1

Template options & placement for The Sampler Quilt (page 16) & In The Woods Quilt (page 50)

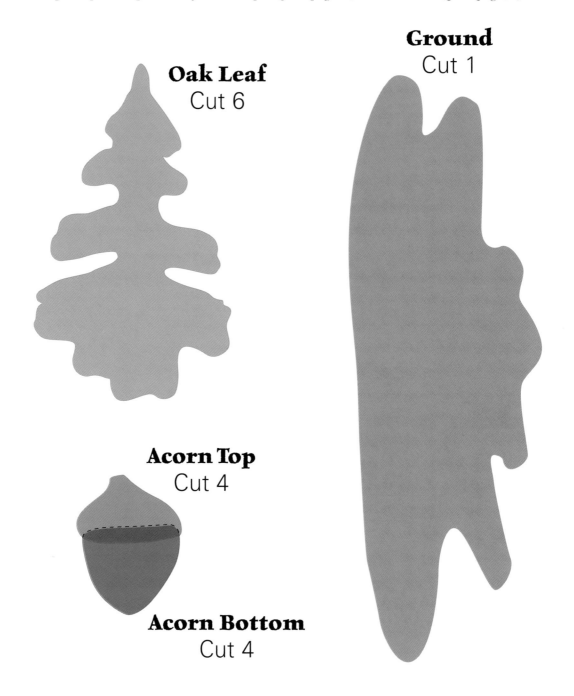

Oak Leaf
Cut 6

Ground
Cut 1

Acorn Top
Cut 4

Acorn Bottom
Cut 4

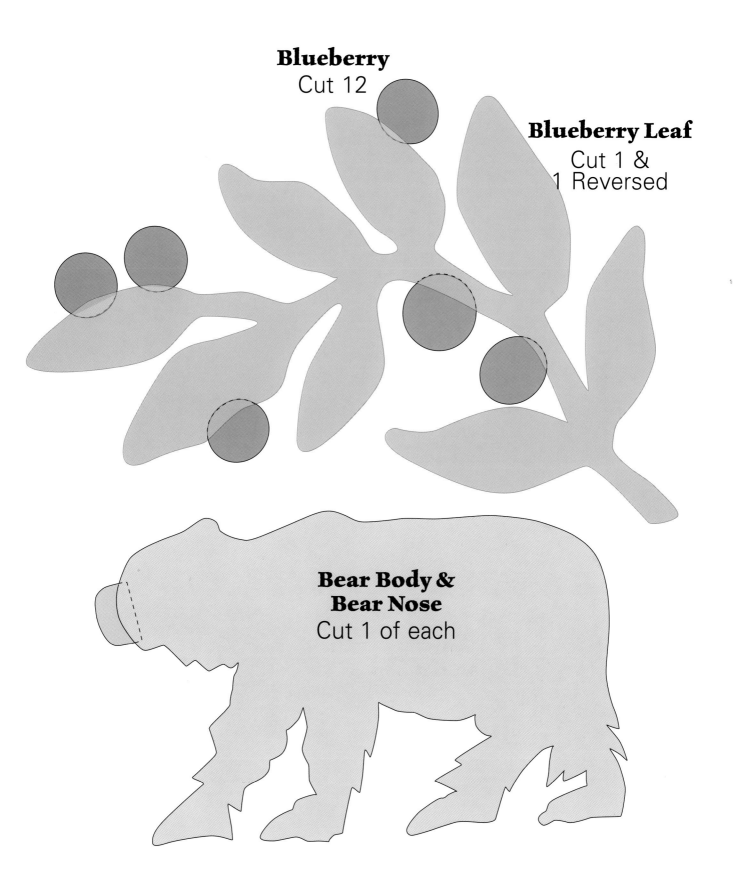

Blueberry
Cut 12

Blueberry Leaf
Cut 1 &
1 Reversed

**Bear Body &
Bear Nose**
Cut 1 of each

Template options & placement for The Sampler Quilt (page 16) & In The Woods Quilt (page 50)

Pods & Centers
Cut 1 of each

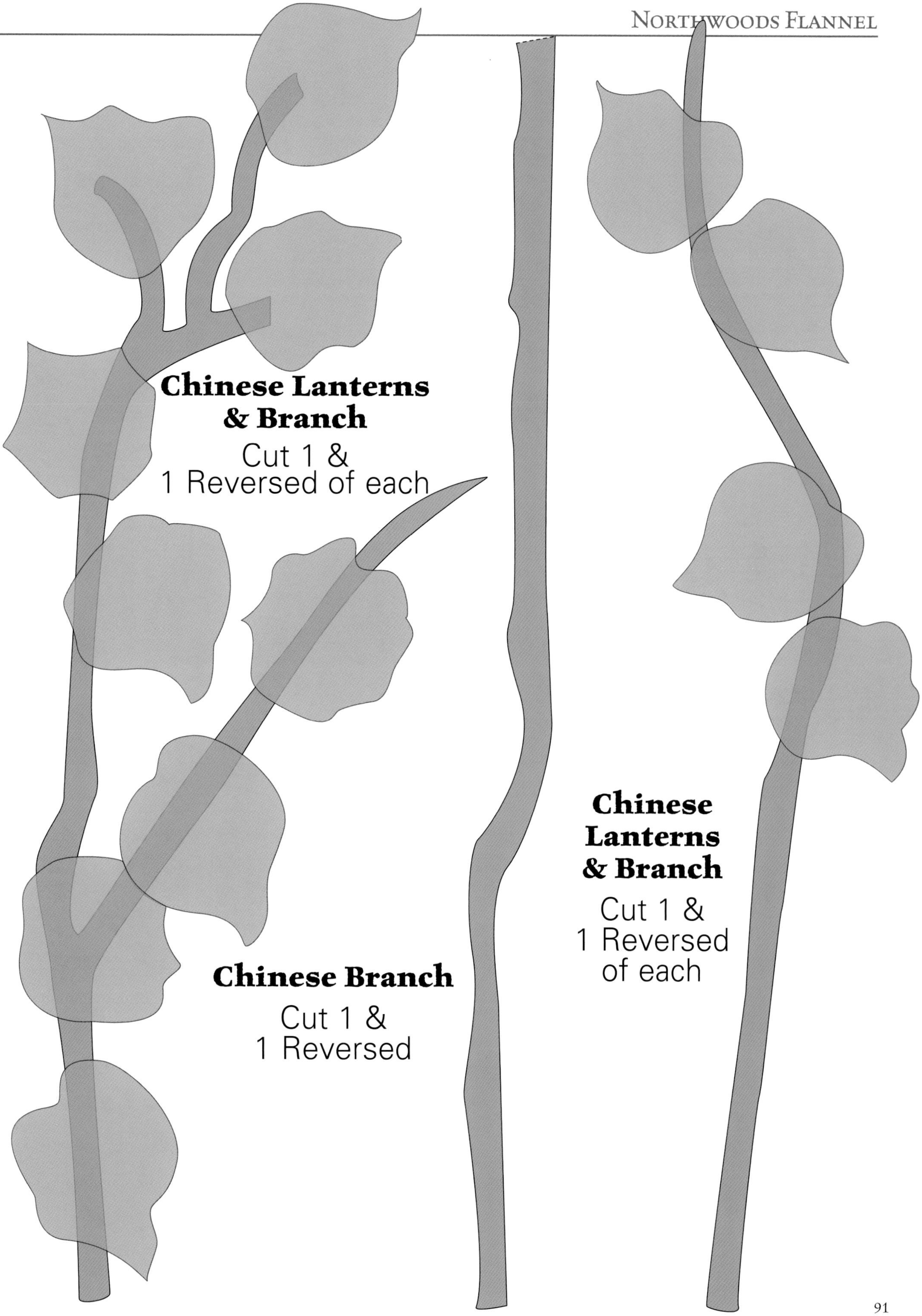

**Chinese Lanterns
& Branch**
Cut 1 &
1 Reversed of each

**Chinese
Lanterns
& Branch**
Cut 1 &
1 Reversed
of each

Chinese Branch
Cut 1 &
1 Reversed

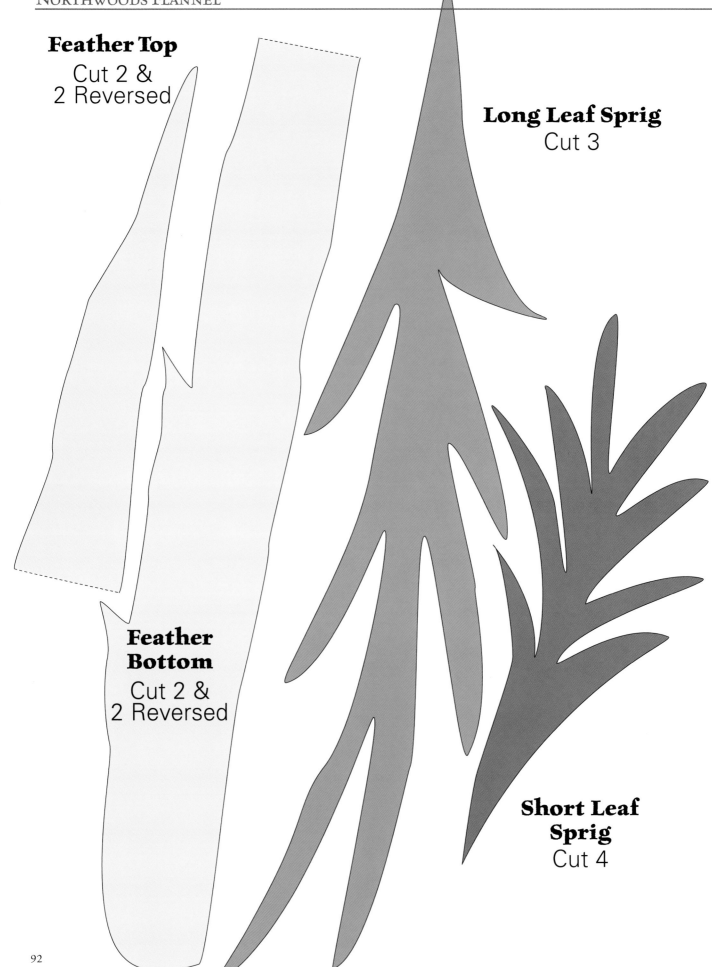

Feather Top
Cut 2 &
2 Reversed

Long Leaf Sprig
Cut 3

**Feather
Bottom**
Cut 2 &
2 Reversed

**Short Leaf
Sprig**
Cut 4

Template options & placement for The Sampler Quilt (page 16) & In The Woods Quilt (page 50)

Tall Tree & Trunk
Cut 4

Short Tree & Trunk
Cut 4

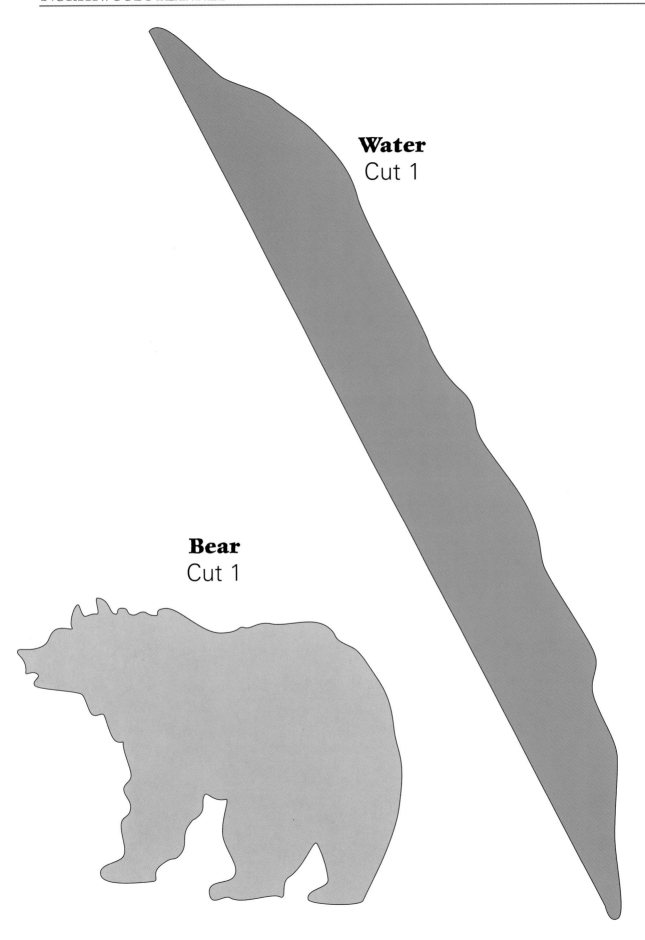

Water
Cut 1

Bear
Cut 1

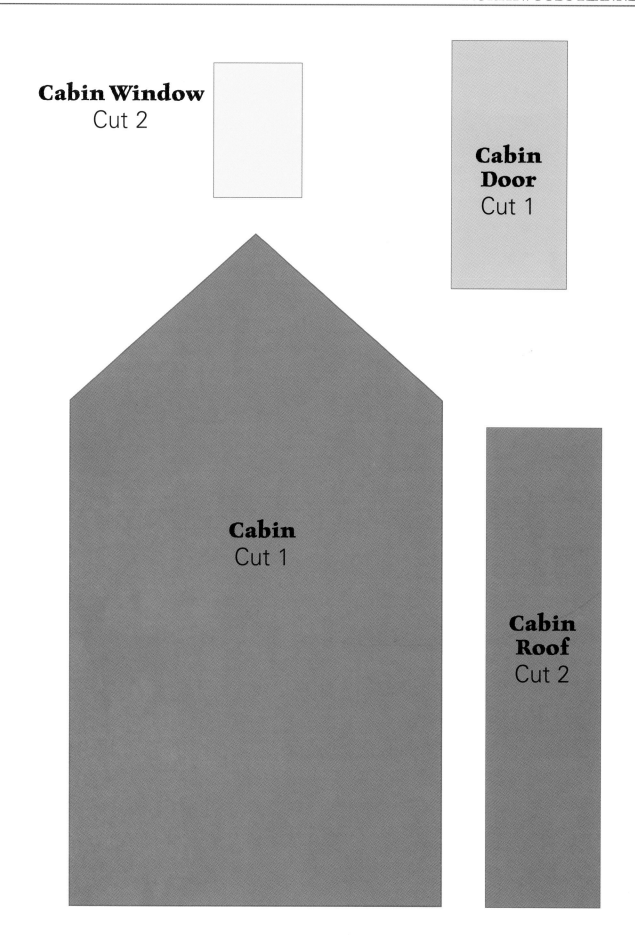

Cabin Window
Cut 2

**Cabin
Door**
Cut 1

Cabin
Cut 1

**Cabin
Roof**
Cut 2

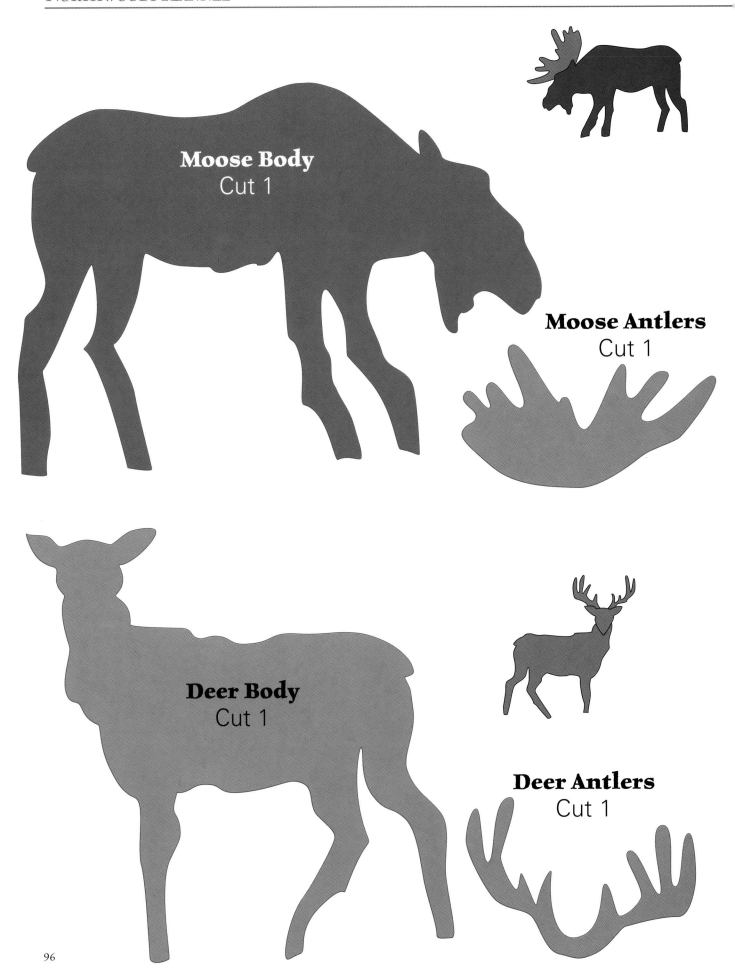

Moose Body
Cut 1

Moose Antlers
Cut 1

Deer Body
Cut 1

Deer Antlers
Cut 1